THE LIBRARY
FLUTE
CLASSICS

WITH SPECIAL THANKS TO VANESSA GIBBONS FOR EDITORIAL ASSISTANCE

ORDER NO. AM 948882
US INTERNATIONAL STANDARD BOOK NUMBER: 0.8256.1707.3
UK INTERNATIONAL STANDARD BOOK NUMBER: 0.7119.7587.6

EXCLUSIVE DISTRIBUTORS:
MUSIC SALES CORPORATION
257 PARK AVENUE SOUTH, NEW YORK, NY 10010 USA
MUSIC SALES LIMITED
14-15 BERNERS STREET, LONDON W1T 3LJ UK
MUSIC SALES PTY. LIMITED
20 RESOLUTION DRIVE, CARINGBAH, NSW 2229, AUSTRALIA

PRINTED IN GREAT BRITAIN

AMSCO PUBLICATIONS
NEW YORK/LONDON/PARIS/SYDNEY

CONTENTS

Scherzino

Joachim Andersen
(1847–1909)

4

Minuet

Johann Sebastian Bach
(1685–1750)

Gavotte

Johann Sebastian Bach
(1685–1750)

Allegro moderato

Trio
Scherzando

Sonata No. 2
(Second Movement)

Johann Sebastian Bach
(1685–1750)

Brandenburg Concerto No. 4
(Theme from First Movement)

Johann Sebastian Bach
(1685–1750)

Brandenburg Concerto No. 5
(Theme from Third Movement)

Johann Sebastian Bach
(1685–1750)

Symphony No. 4
(Theme from Second Movement)

Ludwig van Beethoven
(1770–1827)

Symphony No. 7
(Theme from First Movement)

Ludwig van Beethoven
(1770–1827)

Symphony No. 9
(Theme from Third Movement)

Ludwig van Beethoven
(1770–1827)

Serenade

(Excerpt)

Ludwig van Beethoven
(1770–1827)

Minuet in G

Ludwig van Beethoven
(1770–1827)

TRIO

Minuet D.C.

Symphonie Fantastique

(Theme from First Movement)

Hector Berlioz
(1803–1869)

Habañera
from *Carmen*

Georges Bizet
(1838–1875)

Concerto in D Major
(Theme from Rondeau)

Luigi Boccherini
(1743–1805)

Waltz

Johannes Brahms
(1833–1897)

Symphony No. 1
(Theme from Fourth Movement)

Johannes Brahms
(1833–1897)

Symphony No. 4

(Solo from Fourth Movement)

Johannes Brahms
(1833–1897)

Minute Waltz

Frédéric Chopin
(1810–1849)

SHIP
TO:

ROXINE WILLIAMS

3700 WATERWHEEL RD

EMMETT

ID   83617

US

FULFILLMENT CENTER

251 Mt. Olive Church Road
Commerce, GA 30599

ORDER NO.	PAGE NO.
45196424540572	1 of 1

SHIPMENT NO.	SHIP VIA	DATE
ETZ01839920	USPS	08/25/16

Item Number	SHIP	Line	Item Description	Ord	Purchase Order No.
9780825617072	1	2235908!	The Library of Flute Classics	1	45196424540572

Your satisfaction is our #1 priority, so we make it simple for you: 30 Day, from shipping date, money back guarantee-100% refund on the item purchased. To be eligible for a refund, you must return the item in the same condition you received it - Videos, DVD's, audio, and computer software purchases, returned in the original packaging will receive a 100% item refund. Video, DVD's, audio, and computer software purchases, returned opened and not in the original packaging are non-refundable. Shipping fees are non-refundable.

In order to receive your refund, please use the return label below and enclose this packing slip stating the reason for your return with the items that you are returning. Send the item(s) back to us so we receive them undamaged within 30 days of shipping. We do not accept packages marked return to sender. Postage fees incurred due to packages sent return to sender, refused, undeliverable or deemed to have an insufficient address by the carrier will be deducted from the buyers refund. Shipping and handling charges, for returning the item, are the responsibility of the buyer. A 20% restocking fee will be assessed to all items received returned after 30 days of ship date.

Please ship all returns to:

Fulfillment Center
Ref:[transaction or order number]
251 Mt. Olive Church Road
Commerce, GA 30599

**Tips for returning: Be sure to purchase tracking and/or insure when shipping your package! That way if it is lost or damaged you will still get money back from the shipping company. Also, please allow your return enough mail delivery time to reach us within the 30 day period.

Return Label

VIA: **TLBM**

SHIPPER NO.
PKG. ID# 924909999842881416099

ORDER #   45196424540572

Fulfillment Center
Dept R
251 Mt. Olive Church Road
Commerce, GA 30599

Nocturne

Frédéric Chopin
(1810–1849)

Prelude to the Afternoon of a Faun

Claude Debussy
(1862–1918)

43

Très lent et très retenu jusqu'à la fin

Rêverie

Claude Debussy
(1862–1918)

Ah! So Pure

from *Martha*

Friedrich von Flotow
(1812–1883)

Humoresque

Antonín Dvořák
(1841–1904)

Berceuse
from *Jocelyn*

Benjamin Godard
(1849–1895)

Légende Pastorale

from *Scotch Scenes*

Benjamin Godard
(1849–1895)

Andante quasi adagio

Minuet and Dance of the Blessed Spirits

from *Orfeo ed Euridice*

Christoph Willibald von Gluck
(1714—1787)

Minuet

Andante (♩ = 69)

Dance of the Blessed Spirits

D. C. Minuet

Sonata No. 2

George Frideric Handel
(1685–1759)

Andante M.M. ♩ = 112

Sonata No. 5
(Fourth Movement)

George Frideric Handel
(1685–1759)

Cradle Song

Miska Hauser
(1822–1887)

Serenade

Franz Joseph Haydn
(1732–1809)

Trio No. 4

Franz Joseph Haydn
(1732–1809)

Spring Song

Felix Mendelssohn
(1809–1847)

On Wings of Song

Felix Mendelssohn
(1809–1847)

Scherzo
from *A Midsummer Night's Dream*

Felix Mendelssohn
(1809–1847)

Barcarolle
from *Tales of Hoffman*

Jacques Offenbach
(1819–1880)

Quartet in D
(Second Movement)

Wolfgang Amadeus Mozart
(1756–1791)

Concerto No. 2

Wolfgang Amadeus Mozart
(1756–1791)

Andante ma non troppo

Allegro

Andalouse

Emile Pessard
(1843–1917)

Più moto

Arioso

Johann Joachim Quantz
(1697–1773)

Song of India

Nikolai Rimsky-Korsakov
(1844–1908)

Flight of the Bumblebee

Nikolai Rimsky-Korsakov
(1844—1908)

Melody in F

Anton Rubinstein
(1829–1894)

Scheherazade

Nikolai Rimsky-Korsakov
(1844–1908)

Symphony No. 5

Franz Schubert
(1797–1828)

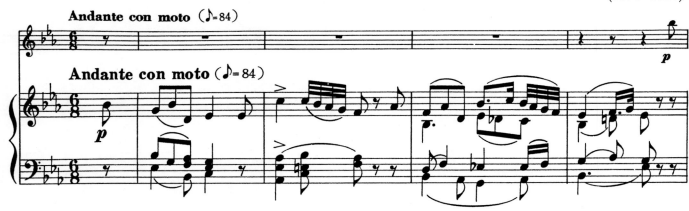

The Swan
from *Carnival of the Animals*

Camille Saint-Saëns
(1835–1921)

Air de Ballet

Camille Saint-Saëns
(1835–1921)

None but the Lonely Heart

Peter Ilyich Tchaikovsky
(1840–1893)

Dance of the Mirlitons
from *The Nutcracker Suite*

Peter Ilyich Tchaikovsky
(1840–1893)

Symphony No. 4
(Theme from First Movement)

Peter Ilyich Tchaikovsky
(1840–1893)

Piano Concerto No. 1
(Theme from Second Movement)

Peter Ilyich Tchaikovsky
(1840–1893)

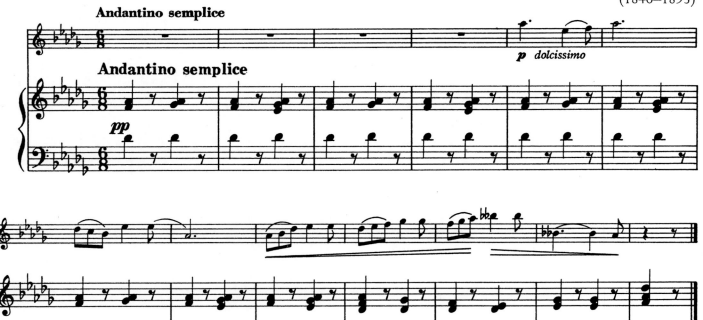

Symphony No. 6
(Theme from First Movement)

Peter Ilyich Tchaikovsky
(1840–1893)

Barcarolle

"June" from *The Seasons*

Peter Ilyich Tchaikovsky
(1840–1893)

Italian Air
from *Suite in A Minor*

Georg Philipp Telemann
(1681–1767)

La Paloma

Sebastián Yradier
(1809–1865)